Juggling on a High Wire

*The Art of Work-Life Balance When
You're Self-Employed*

LAURA POOLE

Juggling on a High Wire: The Art of Work-Life Balance When You're Self-Employed

Published by More Cowbell Books, LLC

Available from Amazon.com, CreateSpace.com, and other retail outlets

ISBN-10: 0986053821
ISBN-13: 978-0-9860538-2-5

Please contact Jake@MoreCowbellBooks.com or write to
More Cowbell Books, 2942 N. 24th St., Suite 114-404, Phoenix, AZ, 85016.

Book design and cover illustration by Jane Gerke

This publication has been compiled based on personal experience, research, and anecdotal evidence, but it is not intended to replace legal, financial, or other professional advice or services. Every reasonable attempt has been made to provide accurate content, and the author and publisher disclaim responsibility for any errors or omissions contained herein. The samples provided are for educational and discussion purposes only. All website addresses cited were current at the time of publication. Any trademarks, service marks, product names, or named features are assumed to be the property of their respective owners and are used solely for editorial reference, not endorsement. It is the reader's responsibility to tailor the content to his or her own business model, experience level, subcontractors, projects, market, and other factors.

DEDICATION

To Katharine O'Moore-Klopf—
mentor, co-presenter, role model, and friend—
with tremendous love and gratitude.

CONTENTS

Preface   vii

Introduction   ix

PART 1   **THE FUNDAMENTALS (Balance, Time, Space)**

Chapter 1   What Is Life Balance?   3

Chapter 2   Task Management   9

Chapter 3   Working from Home   17

Chapter 4   When Your Life Partner Is Also Self-Employed   27

PART 2   **CARING FOR OTHERS AND YOURSELF**

Chapter 5   Working at Home When You Have Kids   35

Chapter 6   Working and Caring for Elderly Parents   51

Chapter 7   Making Time and Space for You   55

PART 3:   **BALANCE CORRECTION**

Chapter 8   Planning Ahead for Work Emergencies   65

Chapter 9   When You're Overworked   71

Chapter 10   When You're Underworked   77

Conclusion   81

Acknowledgments   83

About the Author   85

PREFACE

I'd given the keynote presentation at a conference of writers and editors in upstate New York in 2014, and spent the remainder of the day bouncing around to various breakout sessions. After dinner—given the three-hour time-zone difference from my home base of Phoenix—it felt like it was still early evening for me, even though most of the attendees had packed it in for the night.

I spied Laura Poole, who'd co-presented on work-life balance in one of the day's sessions, and twisted her arm to stay up just a little bit longer. Happily, she agreed.

Over a ginger ale (hers) and a beer (mine), we chatted about freelancing, business, and life in general. It soon struck me that she had one of the more diverse business backgrounds of writers and editors I've known, and we were kindred spirits as far as entrepreneurial philosophy. Not much later, it occurred to us both that her presentation on work-life balance would make a fantastic book.

Whether you're just starting out in self-employment or have been at it for years, you'll surely recognize yourself in the challenges and anecdotes compiled in this volume. More important is the reason I'm proud to have Laura as the first Dr. Freelance Advisor: I'm confident that you can benefit from the strategies she has outlined.

Let's face it, at least part of the reason you became an entrepreneur or freelancer was the promise of freedom. So hop up on that high wire, start juggling…and realize that you can create your own safety net!

—Jake Poinier
September 2015

INTRODUCTION

"Self-employment will be great! I'll work when I want to, then have fun with my friends and family when I want to!" Does that sound familiar? Perhaps you had a similar thought when you were contemplating or starting your freelance career. Before long, you probably had a reality check: "If I'm working 'when I want to,' why does that mean I'm working *all the time*? What happened to spending time with family and friends? Why am I so worn out?"

This book is intended for all freelancers and self-employed people who seek to create a work-life balance that supports all their wants and needs. It's not about "having it all," fitting everything in, or doing more in less time. It's about crafting the life you want to live. Thus, life balance is a very personal, individual vision. This book presents some big-picture tools to help you develop the vision of what you want your work and life to be like, and then outlines some techniques and ideas for helping build it.

I write from my own experience, often borrowing the collective wisdom of a multitude of other freelancer and self-employed colleagues. Eighteen years ago, I quit my job at the tender age of twenty-four to be a full-time freelance copy editor. Like all freelancers and many self-employed people, I've weathered the feast-or-famine cycle of work, bitten off more than I could chew, gained and lost clients, been greatly overworked now and then, and sweated through slower times with minimal paying work. I bought a house, got married, and started a family, all while working in my business. I've connected with countless others who have similar experiences—and similar struggles maintaining a good life while creating a business that requires more attention than we initially thought it would. I share some of my own choices here, not because I'm a role model but because I know my own experience best.

In 2007 I started training to become a certified professional coach (I completed the training in 2009 and was later credentialed by the

International Coach Federation). The concepts of looking at one's whole life and making values-based choices informed how I looked at work-life balance from then on. I've used those techniques to help others evaluate where change needs to happen and to identify the big-picture goals that should guide day-to-day choices. I've coached or mentored quite a few freelancers over the years, and you'll find some insights from those conversations in these pages.

The book is arranged in three major parts. Part 1 covers the fundamentals: concepts of balance (chapter 1), task and time management (chapter 2), and working space (chapter 3). Chapter 4 covers the case when two partners both work from home (a more common arrangement than you might think). Part 2 discusses caring for others: children (chapter 5), elderly parents (chapter 6), and yourself (chapter 7). Part 3 covers balance correction, for those times when work-life balance is way out of whack: planning for emergencies (chapter 8), coping with being overworked (chapter 9), and a useful chapter on things to do when you're underworked and find yourself in a business lull (chapter 10).

My hope is that you'll be inspired to imagine the balance you want, implement the techniques that are relevant for you (or make up some new ones), grow your business, and create the life you dreamed of. Be bold, make changes, and thrive!

—Laura Poole
September 2015

Part 1

THE FUNDAMENTALS
(Balance, Time, Space)

This part covers the definition of life balance, task and time management, and working effectively from a home office. These are the pillars of creating work-life balance. You must think about what your vision of a balanced life is and commit to creating it. Time and task management are not the same as life balance but can help you make choices in how to spend your energy. Many freelancers work from home, and setting up a supportive work space can help you maintain the balance you seek.

CHAPTER 1

What Is Life Balance?
Basic Definitions

Before we go into any detail about balancing work and life, it will be useful to talk about what life balance (or work-life balance) is. It's tempting to think of it like fine art—"I know it when I see it!" A little clarity in terms will be helpful.

Let's start with what life balance is not. Balance is *not*
- fitting everything into your schedule
- saying yes to everything
- spending exactly equal time on work and family
- trying to accomplish more and more

It is not time management (although time management can be a useful tool to support good balance; see chapter 2). Work-life balance is not something you achieve once and lock into forever. Constant course correction is needed!

The best definition of life balance I've ever read was from *Co-Active Coaching*, and it states that "ultimately, balance is about making choices: saying yes to some things and no to others."[1] We often want to say yes to everything—we feel guilty saying no (women, particularly). But if we say yes to everything, obviously we can become overwhelmed, stressed out, and unable to do much of anything. Life balance (and business success)

---

[1] Laura Whitworth, Karen Kimsey-House, Henry Kimsey-House, and Phillip Sandahl, *Co-Active Coaching*, 2nd ed. (Davies-Black, 1998), p. 9.

is not about adding more and more and more to our schedule, and this is where saying yes and no becomes critically important.

Key Point

Ultimately, balance is about making choices:
saying yes to some things and no to others.

Thus, the key to creating a workable life balance is knowing when to say yes and when to say no. I use a set of questions that help guide me when evaluating a new opportunity, assignment, or responsibility.

> **I ask myself:**
> - **If I say yes to this, what else am I saying yes to? What am I saying no to?**
> - **If I say no to this, what else am I saying no to? What am I saying yes to?**

These questions may seem overly simple at first glance, but they lead to profound answers, far beyond just "Do I want to do this?" or lists of pros and cons. Your values will start to show up. If you say yes, you can do so with a whole heart, fully committing. If you say no, you can do so without guilt or apology because you know it's the right thing to do. Saying no from a place of wholeness and positivity is a powerful thing!

For example, I used to volunteer regularly at a local classical music station, every time they had a call-in fund-raiser. At the time, I listened to the station a lot while working, and I like giving time to help out, even when it took a significant portion of a workday. After a few years, I realized I was agreeing to volunteer only because I felt guilty saying "no"—even though I no longer listened to the station! I was able to decline the next request to volunteer and reclaim a bit of my schedule, and I didn't feel guilty about it.

Challenge

Look at an obligation you already have and ask yourself the yes/no questions. Is that obligation something you want to keep up with, something you can recommit to? Or is it time to let it go and make room in your life for something else?

CREATE THE VISION

Life balance is subjective. The definition varies from person to person, and every individual has a different ideal balance, which changes over the life span. I recommend that you set aside some time now and then to create (and sometimes revise) *your* vision of the life and work you want.

Ask yourself:
- What does a balanced life look like to *me*?
- What's my vision of how I *want* to work and live?
- What larger life goals need to be accounted for in that vision?
- Other than work obligations and the necessities of living, what do I want room for in my life?
- What would change in my life if I'm living and working in this vision?
- Who else would be affected?

Key Point

Life balance is all about how *you* want to spend your time and energy.

When creating this vision, think about your values, the core ideals that are most important to you. These are the things (or rather, qualities) that you have to have in your life to feel fulfilled—such as community, integrity, leadership, solitude, connection/bonding, romance and partnership, learning, nurturing, time in nature, and so on. If you can identify your top five or so values and check in on how well you are getting them, you'll be able to quickly identify that when you feel happy and well balanced, when you are "living a value" in a good way.[2] If you feel cranky, out of sorts, or out of balance, you'll be able to tell which of your core values are not being honored. Then you can take steps to bring more of those values into your daily life, correcting your balance.

> **EXAMPLE:** My coaching client Alina was frustrated. She felt like she was working a reasonable amount, still meeting her family obligations, and spending time in her church, something that was important to her. She was exercising regularly and eating well, but she felt down and couldn't pinpoint why, and she didn't know what to do about it. I challenged her to think about her top values, something we had worked on identifying. I asked her: "Which (if any) of these values are you not getting right now? Which one, if you increased it a little bit, would make the rest of your life a little better?" She looked at her list and immediately spotted the problem: one of her values was "time in nature/outdoors," and she hadn't had any significant time for that in weeks. On the spot, she decided to make time for a hike on the weekend. She was visibly cheered and more relaxed when she made the realization and decision.

Also important in crafting the vision of life balance is to occasionally take stock of your life and figure out what no longer fits into that vision. Is there an obligation that's draining your time and energy and no longer serving you? Perhaps it's time to let that go (if you're able

---

[2]You can search for "values finder" and look for coaching-related websites that will help you identify and clarify your values. You can use knowledge of your deepest values as a compass to set goals and create the life you want.

to do so—not all obligations can be shed). Have you come through a major life change that has shaken up your vision? Time to make some changes and dream again.

Sometimes, to create the life balance you want, you'll have to make some key business decisions—such as going after high-paying work so you can work fewer hours or no longer working with clients who drain your energy and goodwill.

Challenge

Identify some key business changes you can make right now that might support you in creating the work-life balance you want.

SELF-TALK AND LIFE BALANCE

Are you sabotaging your chances for a good balance with your own self-talk? Are gremlin voices keeping you stuck, guilting you into taking on more and more because you feel obligated?

Freelancers tend to say yes to whatever our clients ask of us, because "yes" equals a paycheck! Thus, we train ourselves to accept anything and everything that comes our way, sometimes bending over backward to make clients happy. This may be necessary in the early days of being self-employed or as a full-time freelancer, but you will likely overbook yourself regularly or become chronically overworked (and unhealthy) because you're doing too much. If you want to do the work that is most meaningful to you, you have to draw the line somewhere and say no sometimes. If you want a work-life balance that lets you live how you want to, then you must learn to say no.

Quick Tip

Ban the words "should" and "ought to" from your
self-talk vocabulary. Instead of thinking "I should do this"
or "I ought to do that" and allowing that to guilt you into
taking on something that doesn't serve you,
try the yes/no questions. A colleague once said,
"You can 'should' all over yourself"—and it's true!

Have you ever uttered or thought the phrase "I'm a people person!"? These people seem to have the most trouble saying no, even when it's patently necessary to do so. They don't like to let others down. Anecdotal evidence among my peers is that women are particularly reluctant to say no in work situations.

Think of yourself as a people *person*, not a people *pleaser*. You can't please everyone, and you shouldn't try to. Saying no makes it more meaningful when you say yes.

Resources

Matthew Kelly, *Off Balance: Getting Beyond the Work-Life Balance Myth to Personal and Professional Satisfaction* (Hudson Street Press, 2011).

A. Roger Merrill and Rebecca Merrill, *Life Matters: Creating a Dynamic Balance of Work, Family, Time, and Money* (McGraw-Hill Education, 2004).

Andrea Molloy, *Stop Living Your Job, Start Living Your Life: 85 Simple Strategies to Achieve Work/Life Balance* (Ulysses Press, 2005).

CHAPTER 2

Task Management

Task management doesn't equal life balance, but it can support you in creating it. If you have a lot to do, you want to get it done effectively! If you have back-burner projects that you want to do "someday," time and task management can help make them happen. This chapter contains some basic task management tips and concepts (there are plenty of other systems and books out there that get more specific).

Note that I use the phrase "task management" instead of "time management." That's because time isn't really manageable—it marches ahead for everyone at a fixed rate. How you make use of that time is where task management comes into play.

Some task management is about being productive and getting things done, which is particularly important for freelancers. To make a good living, you have to maximize your working time so that you're not constantly running behind.

Dr. Freelance's *Freelance Forecast* survey asks respondents, "What's your favorite aspect of freelancing?" Consistently, "time flexibility" is in the top five responses.

Respondents' tips for freelancers include "Manage your time wisely." Some indicate that "managing time really effectively" is a challenge in their business.

On the flip side of time flexibility comes the temptation to work too hard. When asked about the one thing they dislike most about freelancing, one survey respondent commented: "As a recovering workaholic, I struggle to carve out time for family, friends, and fun."

"I love setting my own schedule and having more time off than I did as an employee."

"My favorite aspect of freelancing is the family-friendly schedule."

USING A CALENDAR OR PLANNER

If you use a digital or day planner (and not everyone does), writing down the tasks and appointments means that your planner will remember for you, so you don't have to be anxious about remembering all the things you need to do. Whether you prefer a monthly, weekly, or daily view, you can use a planner to keep on top of your tasks and get an overview of how you are spending your time. This can be enlightening! Every now and then, conduct a time audit and notice where you have overextended yourself or neglected other needs and values. Then use that information to make changes.

Quick Tip

Before the end of each day or workday, take one minute to review the calendar for at least the next day, if not the next week. Then you'll be prepared for any early-morning appointments, looming deadlines, and changes that need to be made. (I speak from experience. I can't tell you how many doctor appointments I missed first thing on Monday morning because I didn't review my calendar on Sunday night!) If you make daily to-do lists, you'll want to make them the night before (see later discussion), and you can combine that with a calendar review.

If you want a vacation, you may find you need to schedule it (and book it!) a few months in advance. It is easy to accept so much work that you never get time off. Plan your vacation *well* in advance so you can take it, and be sure to tell your clients when you are not available. Be prepared to take some work with you from time to time. No one pays you to take time off when you're self-employed. Frequently, a "vacation" means working half-days at the beach!

DON'T PRIORITIZE THE SCHEDULE, SCHEDULE THE PRIORITIES!

This is the central tenet in Steven Covey, A. Roger Merrill, and Rebecca R. Merrill's excellent book *First Things First*. You don't simply rank-order your tasks, you put the *priorities* on the schedule. Is it important to spend time with your kids? Then write it on the calendar ("Kids home") even if there is nothing specific planned ("Goof-off time with Mom").[1] Feeling overwhelmed? Make sure to schedule some time for enjoyable activities. If it goes on the calendar with all the other tasks, it becomes a higher priority, and not something you push to the back burner for "when you have time."

BLOCKS OF TIME

When I was in direct sales, I learned a lot about effective time management in broad terms. One of my favorite techniques was to categorize portions of a day (or a whole day) to spend time in one or more of the following three categories:

- **Free time**, spent on non-work-related things, which could include time off (vacation), cleaning, errands, doctor visits, hobbies, family time, and more.

- **Focus time**, during which you do those tasks that bring in the money; your billable time.

- **Support time**, during which you work on the business but not generating revenue: taking care of paperwork, follow-up, networking, emails, social media updates, cleaning up the office, and so on.

---

[1] Covey, Merrill, and Merrill also offer a powerful matrix for thinking about your tasks in terms of urgency and importance as well as categorizing your time by the roles you fill (parent, child, business owner, employee, etc.). I highly recommend their book.

Key Point

Set aside time for yourself.
You are important!

You can plan your days with blocks of time that can be flexible. For instance, if your free time is interrupted by an urgent client phone call or a last-minute teleconference, then you might borrow some time out of your support (or even focus) time later.

One of my favorite techniques for getting irritating work done involves smaller *time chunks*. If you have a task that seems so huge you can't even get started, try setting a timer for fifteen minutes (or ten, or even just five). Work at it until the timer goes off, and then you can stop and do something else.

This works amazingly well because the time chunk is small enough that you can get started and just get it out of the way, and you have permission to quit at the end of it. It fits any schedule well—you can set a daily goal of "at least three time chunks on Task A today" and then break the task up into slots where it fits.

Many people are surprised at just how much they can get done in fifteen minutes. Sometimes they finish the whole task in the first chunk! Other times, just getting started gives them the momentum to keep going to the end (many people will keep going after the timer stops, because they have made more progress than they thought they would).

This technique also works fabulously for cleaning the house, especially if you want the whole family to help out. "OK, everybody cleans for ten minutes!"

TAKE ADVANTAGE OF YOUR
MOST PRODUCTIVE TIME OF DAY

What are your natural body rhythms? Are you an early riser or more of a night owl? Do you have an after-lunch mental slump (devolving into nap time), or do you get your second wind after dinner? Observe yourself and pay attention to when you are most effective, and try to reserve that time as when you do your billable work.

For instance, I am an early riser. I am most effective and clearheaded first thing in the morning, so on very busy days, I get up extra early—as early as 5:30 a.m.—to get more work done. I find that in the hour or ninety minutes I have to work before the rest of the family wakes up around 7:00, I can get a surprising amount of work done—sometimes equaling three hours' worth of work later in the day. This scheduling has allowed me to be more productive in reduced hours while my daughter is very young.

On the flip side, mid- to late afternoon is my slow-brain period, so I reserve that time for other business tasks and errands (or even a nap!) whenever possible.

DELETE, DEFER, DELEGATE

If you are overwhelmed with tasks and not sure how to proceed, you may have to implement the three D's. Look at your tasks and appointments and evaluate whether you can delete, defer, or delegate.

Delete: For some reason, this is the hardest thing for us to do with our tasks (it's much easier to defer everything). Take a clear-eyed look at your planner and task list. Too much to do? Cancel your coffee or lunch date if you have to. Skip the networking meeting this week. Remove from your list the things you can honestly do without. Refuse to feel guilty for deleting them.

Defer: It's tempting to defer *everything* on your list (it's easier on our consciences), but you should defer until later only those things that you want to keep and still do. Do you have three deadlines on the same day? Perhaps you could call your clients and find out if at least one can be moved a bit later. Maybe that coffee date you deleted should really be deferred (after all, renewing friendships is important, too). If you defer something more than a few times, you need to either make it a priority and be done with it, or delete it because it just isn't happening.

Delegate: Possibly harder than deleting a task is delegating it to someone else. Can you let go of the task and trust someone else to handle it without supervision? If you can do this where necessary, you'll free up time and mental energy for the things that matter. Delegating can include using an assistant (virtual or on site), a cleaning service, a babysitter, or a CPA, or even just assigning your kids more chores and responsibilities around the house.

TO-DO LISTS

Some people thrive by using to-do lists as a way to keep tasks organized and top of mind. Like using a planner, you write things down on a list so that the list remembers for you, and you don't have to fret about remembering little details. (Many people use both planners and lists!) I am a fan of a daily to-do list, and several techniques work well for helping you get more done.

Tip 1: Keep the list short. A daily to-do list should be no more than five to ten items. You can certainly keep a master task list if you have more than that, but a daily list should be short and achievable. Too many items on the list seems to inspire the attitude of "Well, I can't do it all, so I won't even start." A long list can be quite intimidating! Keep it manageable. Anything that doesn't get done gets carried over to the next day's list. The list can have a mix of lengthy tasks and shorter tasks (e.g., "Call doc for appointment / Write next blog post / Start data analysis programming").

Tip 2: Make the daily list the night *before.* It's astonishing how much you can get done if you make your list of top priorities on the day before you need to do them. (I like to combine this list-making with a one-minute calendar review to see what appointments might be coming up.) Your subconscious brain works on things overnight. The very first time I tried making a day-before list, I thought, "Well, I'll be lucky if I do three of these six things by the end of the day." I was pleasantly shocked to accomplish four of them by noon the next day!

Tip 3: Put something on the list that's very easy or something you have already done. It sounds silly (and I always gets laughs when I mention this), but if you put down something like "Make list" or "Get coffee" and you can cross it off right away, you have momentum! The rest of the list doesn't look so bad because you have already accomplished one of the items.

BEING PRODUCTIVE DURING YOUR WORK TIME

To protect the time you spend away from work, you'll need to be sure to be productive during your working hours. There are whole books and websites on productivity techniques (see the Resources section), so I won't get into those concepts in detail here. Instead, here are a few tips in general terms.

- If you work from home (and many self-employed people do), you'll need to set up your home office to support you physically and mentally. See chapter 3 for more ideas.

- Check the background noise! If you need quiet, consider noise-canceling headphones. If you like to listen to tunes, pick music that won't distract you or can help you focus. For instance, I'm a book editor, so I work with words all day. I can't listen to music with lyrics in English, because they distract me, so I listen to orchestral, classical, New Age, ambient, or Celtic music. Symphonic minimalist music (particularly compositions by Philip Glass) help me get in a particularly focused state of mind. Sometimes I want something a lot more upbeat if my energy is dragging, so I'll pull out the dance tunes!

- Use your most productive time of day for billable work. I mentioned that earlier in this chapter, and it bears repeating here. When you're a freelancer, you are in business for yourself, and you will need to spend some time getting more business (work *on* the business). Make sure your best time of day is devoted to the work that brings in the money (working *in* the business).

- Limit your time wasters and distractions. Turn off the TV, close the email window, ignore Facebook and social media if necessary. Do not visit the fridge every twenty minutes or play with your pets every half hour.

Resources

Stephen R. Covey, A. Roger Merrill, and Rebecca R. Merrill, *First Things First* (Franklin Covey, 1996).

Brian Tracy, *Eat That Frog! 21 Great Ways to Stop Procrastinating* and *Get More Done in Less Time* (Berrett-Kohler, 2007).

David Allen's books *Getting Things Done* and *Ready for Anything* (http://gettingthingsdone.com).

The Pomodoro Technique (http://pomodorotechnique.com).

CHAPTER 3

Working from Home

Many self-employed people or freelancers work from home. It's an attractive lifestyle: you can roll out of bed, commute a few steps down the hall to your office, and work in your pajamas all day. No commute, no dress code, and you get a tax break for using your home as work space! Lots of people who work from home find they are much more productive than they would be in an office because they aren't distracted by co-workers, office politics, meetings, and so on. Working from home does have a few pitfalls, though, and we address some of them in this chapter.

Dr. Freelance's *Freelance Forecast* survey asks respondents about what they love about freelancing:

"It allows me to be a stay-at-home mom and a writer without sacrificing either goal."

"Jammies, all day long."

For the question "How important are the following items to your satisfaction as a freelancer?", the response "no commute/I can work from anywhere" consistently ranks "very important."

The survey also asks what they dislike about freelancing:

"People assuming that because I work from home, I'm always available to do things for them."

"Not having people respect what you do and [having them] think because you work at home you have all the time in the world."

THE HOME OFFICE

If you're going to have an office at home, it needs to be a space that can support your work properly. It's tempting to just turn a spare room into an office (or just park your laptop on the dining room table) simply because it's the most convenient option, but I encourage you to give some thought and consideration to your needs and preferences. Work space should support your healthy body and your work style, and ideally not overflow into the house.

- Do you have enough outlets and Internet access (WiFi signal or cables) for computers and other electricity-requiring gadgets?
- Is there enough space for a good desk, bookshelves, and other furniture you might need?
- Do you have enough light (overhead or lamps)?
- Will you need to move around the room, and do you have enough space for it?
- What sort of physical storage space will you need?

You might have to invest in some changes to make your home office appropriate for your work. This can mean, for example, purchasing an ergonomic chair, cleaning and reorganizing the space, or totally remodeling. Keep ergonomics in mind: it's difficult (or impossible) to work when you're in pain, so your work setup should have proper back support, wrist support, and so on.

One of the major downsides of working from home is that you can easily end up working *all the time*. If your work is right there, it's easy to sit down for just "twenty more minutes," which can turn into a few more hours. When deadlines loom and projects are stacked, it's easy to sacrifice your evening and weekend time to working instead of taking a break. Having your office right there at home makes it very easy to overwork yourself. After a while, you get *used* to working all the time, and you start to wonder what happened to that time flexibility that you looked forward to when choosing to work from home.

Key Point

It's easy to end up working all the time
when you work from home.

This is why my recommendation for a home office is to have one dedicated room with a door you can close. Of course, this is not always possible, based on floor plans, size of homes, family needs, and budgets. Do your very best to have separate work space somewhere in your home. It's convenient to have work space "wherever it fits" (even spread across one or more rooms), but it's important to be able to close off your work from your home. This helps you separate these domains in a mental mind-set, which can be key to maintaining life balance.

Key Point

Do your best to keep your home office
in a clear, delineated space, preferably a room
with a door you can close.

The idea of working from home can be appealing because people think they will work "when they want to" or "when they feel like it." The reality is, you can end up working all the time and have few boundaries between work and life—boundaries that you sometimes need to maintain. It's easy to miss this fact until you are so overworked that you're exhausted and can't work anymore. A lot of people who work from home fall into the emotional trap of feeling guilty about not working while spending time with family, but then feeling guilty about not being with family when working! Feeling guilty will derail your life balance because you will probably end up frantically spending more time on both pursuits, which is exhausting and ultimately not sustainable.

Another good reason to have a separate office is that it helps you maintain physical boundaries. You can enforce your work space (as needed) if you can close the door or tell family members, "This is my work space, not your play space/craft space/homework spot." One colleague loves having glass doors on her home office, so she can block out sounds but still glance out and feel connected with the rest of her household. On the flip side of that, it's nice to have space in your home that is simply for living, for being with family, for rest and relaxation—not invaded by work. Even an open doorway between living space and work space can be a guilt-inducing visual reminder that we "ought" to be spending time on something else. Maintaining separate work and living areas helps you keep those boundaries intact. One *2012 Freelance Forecast* respondent said that the most frustrating aspect of freelancing was "maintaining a work/production conducive environment inside my home; making certain [that] day-to-day chores do not interfere with my work."

When you have a separate office with a door you can close, it helps you step into your work space and work mind-set, literally and figuratively. A lot of people find they are most productive when they are mentally ready, and the physical act of stepping into the office can be part of that process. This ties in with the human need for ritual. It's part of the way home workers put on their "work brain" to be productive.

For a variety of reasons, some people don't or can't dedicate a separate room entirely to work.

Words of Wisdom
from Katharine O'Moore-Klopf

I have had my office in my kitchen for almost twenty-one years now. It has been there out of necessity: my house is small, and there are no extra rooms available to be made over into an office. But I have come to love it because after the living room, the kitchen is the most popular room in my home. Everyone pops in now and then to get something to eat or drink, and they stop at my desk to talk. Working in that location, I'm guaranteed to get hugs. When my youngest, now thirteen, comes home from school, I see him immediately because our front door is close to the kitchen. We reconnect after his day at school. My desk is positioned right up against the wall that has windows onto the front yard. I can look up from my computer screens and see birds and wild rabbits. I can see neighbors coming and going. And I get plenty of great sunlight. If my family and I ever do get around to adding onto the house, we'll have to include an office for me that is centrally located so I can see family members frequently and so I can see the world outside big windows.

GUIDELINES AND REGULATIONS

Be sure you're following government regulations and guidelines about working from home. Your life balance will be way out of whack if you get fined or penalized with legal sanctions!

Federal Guidelines: The IRS has somewhat strict standards for being able to take the home office deduction on your taxes. The government requires that the office be used *regularly* and *exclusively* for business. This means if you work on the couch with your laptop one day a month, you cannot write off your living room as a home office because you aren't using it regularly. If you have a "hobby room" and you clear out half to have a workstation (or if you set up a work space in your bedroom), you wouldn't technically qualify for the home office deduction because the room isn't used exclusively for business. Another requirement is that your home must be the *principal place of your business*. Thus, if you rent an outside office but work from home one or two days a week, you can't deduct the home office as well.[1] You do not need to receive clients in your home to qualify for the deduction.

Home office deductions are based on the percentage of square footage of your home (owned or rented) used for your business. If you can dedicate a single room to your business—with a door you can close—then these calculations are a lot easier. Many people think that taking the home office deduction is an automatic ticket to an IRS audit, but this is not the case. I have worked from home for more than fifteen years and never once been audited (and neither has my husband, who is also self-employed).

State and Local Laws: Your state, county, or town may have regulations about working from home or may require a business license, even if you are a sole proprietor. These rules are meant to prevent someone from running a retail store in a residential neighborhood. In some areas you may need a business license (sometimes called a privilege license) to be renewed each year. Obviously, we can't discuss all fifty states and numerous municipalities in this book, so do your own due diligence, research your area, and stay legal!

Key Point

Research your state and local laws about
self-employment and working from home.
Be your own advocate!

When I first began working from home, my town requested a "work from home" permit. It was simply a form to fill out describing the nature of the business, whether clients/customers were seen at the home, and

---

[1] IRS Publication 587, "Business Use of Your Home," has more details. See http://www.irs.gov/publications/p587/index.html.

so on. An inspector came out once the form was received and made sure the business was truly a one-person shop. The permit was free and did not need to be renewed. My county requires a privilege license for all businesses, and it's renewed each year. The fees for this permit are based on the business's gross receipts for the previous year, but aren't very onerous and are simple to calculate.

WORKING IN A NOISY ENVIRONMENT

Even if you have a separate room with a door to close, you may not be able to minimize background noise when you're working. Interior sounds—talking family, phones ringing, ventilation noise, pets—can be distracting. Exterior noise (construction, yard work, loud motorcycles) can intrude. If you need to concentrate, you'll have to find ways to increase your focus by dealing with extraneous noise.

- Invest in a good pair of noise-canceling headphones or earplugs.
- If music or nature sounds help you concentrate, turn them on, at a volume level that isn't too distracting.
- Mute or close all noisy distracting items on your computer when necessary: email notifications, Twitter, Facebook, even your web browser. Or you can relegate these items to a second monitor.
- Plan to do most of your work when family members are out of the house (at work or school).
- Go mobile if you have to on really noisy days at home: take your laptop to the park, to the library, or wherever you can concentrate best.

What if the noisiness is not environmental background but is created by loved ones clamoring for attention? Set limits with household members:

- "When I'm doing such-and-such activity, please don't talk to me."
- "When I'm on deadline, *do not approach me.*"
- "Unless there's blood or fire, don't bother me!"

MANAGING THE EXPECTATIONS OF OTHERS

Just because you work from home doesn't mean you're sitting around eating bonbons all day! Sometimes people may not fully understand that you need work time just as much as anyone who reports to an office at 9:00 a.m. You have more flexibility in your time, which is great, but it is not a privilege to be abused. Educate your family members and friends on your work, your work style, your work hours, and what you need them to do. A writer colleague had to do this after her family would volunteer her (without consulting her) to take an elderly relative to a doctor appointment because "she's not doing anything."

Do you have neighbors dropping by for coffee or to say hello because they know you're home all the time? Do friends constantly call you for a ride to the airport? Do relatives and pals call to chat because they know you're available? You may enjoy and even crave this social time, but do not let it start to interfere with your work. In busy weeks, you may have to cut some of your social appointments, screen phone calls, and not answer the door (better yet, put a sign on the door that you're not interruptible) so you can get work done.

If your spouse works outside the home, they may be surprised that the house isn't sparkling clean and there's no hot dinner on the table when they arrive home after work. Obviously, working from home affords you some flexibility to start a load of laundry or wash a few dishes, but cleaning the house doesn't pay the bills. You have work to be done, and that must take priority during working hours. Talk with your spouse about expectations for housework, cooking, and child care so that your time is respected and everyone's needs are met.

ISOLATION

One of the major downsides of working from home—something that many people have difficulty dealing with—is isolation and even loneliness. Many introverts love working independently from home and find it an ideal situation, but those with extrovert tendencies may find it difficult (or even depressing) at times. If it's important to you to connect with people and get out in the world, you will have to plan for this and build it into your work schedule. You cannot maintain a healthy work-life balance if you feel lonely, sad, or depressed. If connecting with others recharges your mental batteries, then it's important and you should make it happen!

Key Point

Plan to get out of the house on a regular basis.

Cultivate in-person and online friendships so that you can have some fun, have someone to vent to, and have someone to brainstorm work and life solutions with. Virtual communities (and in-person ones!) of other freelancers or people in your industry can be a great way to connect and get some human interaction. Professional groups help you build your business while getting social time and honing networking skills. Regular lunch dates or coffee chats with friends are a helpful way to relieve pressure.

It's far too easy to get so wrapped up in work that we neglect ourselves. If you have family demands on top of work obligations, then you probably know that your own personal needs get pushed to the back burner, sometimes for long stretches. This isn't good for anyone's well-being! Do not be afraid to make *yourself* a priority. Schedule time off, schedule "me time," and don't apologize for it or feel guilty about it. (See chapter 7 for more about making time for you.)

TAKING CARE OF THE HOME

A lot of people swear they could never work from home because they would have to clean everything first. Those of us who actually work from home know the truth: the housework *waits* because washing the dishes doesn't pay the bills. Many people who work from home tip the scales the other way: working all the time and not doing *any* housework, or letting it pile up until it's out of control.

How you choose to take care of your living space while working from home is a very personal approach. I find that a lunch break in which I start a load of laundry, wash some dishes, and maybe tidy for a few minutes can be a great mental break in the middle of the day. Others prefer a big cleanup day now and then.

You can outsource as many household chores and tasks as you want:

- Hire helpers when you have the funds (for child care, housecleaning, yard work, etc.). Delegate tasks when needed!

- Use grocery or pharmacy delivery services so that you can conserve time for relaxation.

- Order takeout when you need to, and don't feel guilty about it.

- Consider cooking in bulk and freezing meals so that you have ready-made food when you get very busy.

It may seem expensive to hire help or use external services, but consider this: if it takes you four hours to clean the house, and a housecleaning service can do it in one, you have just freed up four billable hours to focus on other things!

CHAPTER 4

When Your Life Partner Is Also Self-Employed

I have a work-from-home spouse sharing my office space, and an informal poll among several colleagues revealed that this is a remarkably common arrangement! I thought it important to address the kinds of issues that crop up in dual working-at-home relationships. A lot of people have a rosy view of how great it could be when two lovebirds work from home. The reality can be quite nice at times, but it can also test a relationship in unexpected ways. When you're together *all the time*, it can be stressful on a relationship, especially if one or both of you are introverts. It's easy to start getting snippy with each other or even start fighting.

My husband and I share a single office for our business ventures (he now telecommutes for his full-time job). When we first began working this way, we were concerned about whether we would end up hating each other! Wisely, we set a few handy guidelines that worked well:

- No idle chitchat during the time we are working.
- Respectfully answer the phone for each other if necessary.
- Make sure we have our time away from each other as well.

SET YOURSELVES UP FOR SUCCESS

To get off on the right foot, be sure to talk about the work atmosphere each of you needs to be most productive and how you can accommodate each other. You may need to rearrange things in your home office and agree on what kind of background music you are allowed to play (or whether you should have headphones).

Key Point

Be sensitive to each other in your work space.

Consider keeping a wall (or digital) calendar with certain key things on it: appointments, deadlines, scheduled conference calls or Skype chats, webinars, and so on. This helps you both be aware of work rhythms and when your partner might need a quiet office.

Because your personal lives are entwined, it's easy to forget good office etiquette:

- Respect your partner's mental work space. If you are both at work in the office, be quiet. Work time is not chatting time.

- Respect your partner's physical work space. Don't store your business stuff in your partner's office or portion of a shared office.

- Check with your partner about work-time conflicts before planning business meetings or conference calls.

- Don't swipe your partner's office supplies. Ask first. Better yet, buy your own.

- Know how your partner wants their business phone answered and messages taken, if applicable.

CARVING OUT TIME FOR YOUR RELATIONSHIP

Workaholism because of fear of business dry spells (and thus accepting too many projects) is a problem for many freelancers. To avoid letting this scenario damage your love relationship, consider the following ideas.

- Agree on what time each day you'll stop work. This may vary from time to time, or even be wildly different for each of you (I like to work in the morning; my husband prefers to sleep in and then work later at night).

- Make an effort to eat a meal together every day, and sometimes go out for lunch, away from the home office.

- Schedule date nights or work-free time together so you can see each other as love interests, not just co-workers. Sometimes, taking a walk together for ten minutes as a work break can be a great way to reconnect during a busy week. After a long haul of hard work, a romantic weekend getaway might be just the thing!

- If it's possible to avoid working weekends, try to do so. But your weekends don't have to consist of Saturdays and Sundays.

Key Point

Remember to make your relationship a priority.

WORKING TOGETHER

You can make work life easier if you decide to help each other with specific business tasks:

- Managing your respective business websites. If one of you is better at the back end of web work, maybe that person can maintain both sites. If one of you is better at writing copy, lend a hand!

- Being a second set of eyes on business correspondence or double-checking project estimates and proposals. A fresh review can be just the thing to catch misspellings or soften the occasional harsh word.

- Serving as a sounding board about work issues. Sometimes you need to blow off steam, and other times you need some creative brainstorming.

SPLITTING THE HOUSEWORK

When you both work from home, you'll need to negotiate (and renegotiate as circumstances change) responsibility for household chores. If you have kids, get them involved in regular chores as well. If you have to set aside set times to do housework, then put it on the schedule! Sometimes just fifteen minutes of "Everybody clean!" can be quite effective (see chapter 2 on using time chunks).

CHILD CARE

Many people choose to work from home to have flexibility around parenting their children. If you and your spouse both work from home, agree on who has what child care responsibilities. Who does the school run? Who is responsible when a child is home sick? How flexible can you be with that—does it boil down to the same person all the time, or can it vary based on workload and schedule? (See chapter 5 on working at home with kids at different ages for more details and thoughts.)

MONEY

Discuss how you'll each handle your business's finances and how that will fit in with your personal finances.

- Keep funds and accounts for each business separate. This is crucial for maintaining clear, easy-to-follow records for taxes.

- Separate or joint personal bank accounts? You might have multiple accounts for both. I have a business checking and savings account, personal checking and savings, and joint checking with my husband (who also has separate business and personal accounts). It's a bit convoluted, but it works for our lives and our relationship.

- Who does the mutual personal bookkeeping? Who is responsible for household bills?

- Keep each other informed about major business expenses coming up, because those affect personal income.
- Seriously consider using a CPA or other professional tax preparer. One self-employed person can benefit from a tax preparer, but two in one household almost require the extra help. Doing the books for two businesses *and* calculating personal returns would test any relationship. This is another outsourcing choice that can really pay off. (I always says that a CPA will save you more money than you pay them.)

TIME APART

Even if you love each other dearly and work incredibly well together or independently side by side, at some point you will get tired of seeing each other all day, every day. Preserve your relationship and your sanity by planning regular things to do without your spouse. Get out of the house on your own, have some time with your friends, and spend time on a hobby that doesn't involve your sweetie.

POSTSCRIPT

When I first developed the presentation that led to this book, my co-presenter and I compiled a list of tongue-in-cheek subtitles for this chapter (and then some other colleagues chimed in).

- Quit Hogging the Bathroom
- Stop Working around the Clock and Kiss Your Officemate
- No, You Said *You* Would Watch the Kids
- Put Your Pants On, the UPS Guy Is Delivering My Project
- I'm Undressing for a Shower, Not for Your Entertainment
- Grab the Barking Dog and Shut Him Up—I Have to Take This Client's Call!

- If You Fix My Website, I'll Proofread Your Email
- You Wrote *What* to Your Client?!
- When Did You Say That Client Was Going to Pay You?
- Wake Up, You Have Deadlines!
- Stop "Borrowing" My Phone Charger
- Save Me Some Cake

Part 2

CARING FOR OTHERS AND YOURSELF

This part offers strategies for incorporating your caring obligations and choices with your work schedule. Kids, parents, spouses, and our own selves require regular attention, and everyone thrives when these relationships are well tended. Many freelancers and self-employed people choose to work for themselves specifically to have the flexibility of time to care for others. But then we often end up working much harder than we thought we would need to, leaving precious little energy for other obligations. It's also easy to get into a feast-or-famine work situation in which we're either working super-hard to meet deadlines or have little billable work, instead of a consistent, moderate level of work. This is ultimately exhausting, draining, and even demoralizing. Thinking about your choices in caring for others and the relationships you want to maintain helps guide your choices to create the balance you seek.

CHAPTER 5

Working at Home When You Have Kids

Many people like the flexibility of freelancing and/or working from home because it offers more options for being available for children and family. This is an undeniable appeal for some, but like everything else with working on your own, there are some downsides and difficulties in arranging an optimum balance. Many of my colleagues and I have worked at home with children of various ages, and my industry (publishing) is heavily dominated by women, who tend to be understanding of this work situation. You can craft an excellent balance of work time and family time with a little effort and thought. Be aware that family needs constantly change, and what worked when your kids were in preschool won't necessarily work when they are in junior high!

Key Point
Family needs constantly change.
Be adaptable and flexible as your kids get older.

When I was pregnant with my daughter, I had a few insights that helped make my choices easier and my life as a new parent a bit smoother. Some of them were derived from my experience and training as a professional coach.

Here they are:

- **Let go of any hard-and-firm plans and preconceived notions.** It's nice to have an idea of how and when you will work after a child comes into your life, but in reality, you won't know what your kid needs—or what you need—until you've all gotten to know each other. This is true even for second, third, or more kids. Every child needs something different, and every addition to the family reshapes the family dynamics. I was fortunate to have a child who slept through the night at ten weeks old, so I was well rested and able to pick up work fairly soon. My colleague Katharine O'Moore-Klopf worked with her infant son strapped to her (and now does the same with an infant granddaughter).

- **When choosing if, how, and when to go back to work after a baby is born (or at any point, really), do what's best for *all* of you, not solely what's best for your children to the exclusion of your own needs.** If you need and want to go back to work soon or even right away, that is a valid desire, and you should do it—without apology and without guilt. Your child's needs are very important, of course, but there's no need to sacrifice everything you've built. If your family needs the income or benefits from you working, then that's valid, too. For many working moms, the "working" part keeps the "mom" part sane!

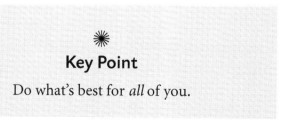

✳ Key Point

Do what's best for *all* of you.

- **Find a middle way.** Too many people perceive "working" as full-time hours only and don't look for part-time schedules, three-quarters time, or other flexible options. There might be ways to arrange your workload so you're doing higher-paying work and don't have to put in as many hours. With support from other family members, creativity in scheduling, and paid child care, you can do as much work as you want while still being available for your kids. It's not the hours between 8:00 a.m. and 5:00 p.m. that make you a mom… or a freelancer. This is where the flexibility of freelancing and working from home really can support you!

INFANTS AND TODDLERS

Can you work with a baby or toddler in your life? Sure you can! But it may well not be at the same level as before you had kids. You will have to make some adjustments to your work style, workload, expectations, and routine. The benefit of being a freelancer or self-employed is that you can continue working, if you choose to, with these adjustments and some help. Obviously, new moms need to take time off for healing and infant care, but that length of time is up to you. New dads also need time to bond with the baby and adjust to the new family dynamics. Having a baby does not necessarily spell the end of your freelance career just because you take time off. As you figure out your child, your changed family routines, and your own needs, you can figure out the work style that is best for you. Some basic tips follow.

Adjust your expectations about how much work you'll get done. After the major change of a new child coming into your life, do not expect to be able to snap back into a regular work schedule like before. Even if you weren't the one to give birth, having a child changes everything. It can be hard to focus mentally, a topsy-turvy schedule can mean working off hours, and lack of sleep can result in general fogginess. Newborns need a lot of time and attention. Toddlers and preschoolers need less intense physical care but may want to be entertained and played with.

Follow a work schedule that works for you and your child. As I mentioned, do what's best for all of you. If your child sleeps late and you are an early riser, get up early and take advantage of that working time.

Work in sprints. Work a while, do some parenting/child care, work a while, do more parenting, and so on. You may need a wide spread of hours to get in enough work spurts. Can you trade off with your spouse? Work while your child is napping? Have a mother's helper or babysitter for a few hours? Take advantage of these opportunities.

Nap when your baby or toddler naps. It's tiring running a business and parenting, especially in your child's first few years. I've just recommended that you work while your child is napping, but keep in mind that if you are exhausted, you won't do good work. Take care of yourself, and make it a priority.

Key Point

Don't push yourself to exhaustion. Taking care of yourself should be a priority.

Keep your business phone set to go directly to voicemail. Then you can respond to calls later when you can be sure you'll have a quiet child. You can restrict yourself to using email only for business, and educate your clients that you may not answer the phone or email right away, but you will get back to them.

Get help with child care. It's not a crime to get help with child care. Sometimes it's a necessity if you want to keep your business running at some level, especially if you have a child who can't or won't self-entertain.

- Consider using either in-home or out-of-home child care, even for just a few hours a week.

- Enlist the aid of friends and relatives for child care.

- Develop a formal or informal child care cooperative with neighbors, trading off time spent providing child care for one another.

- Find a middle way: As I mentioned already, there are more options than just full-time employed or full-time parent. As self-employed people, we can craft a middle-way solution that many people don't have the luxury of finding.

My Middle Way

When my daughter was born, I found another freelancer to help my clients while I was out of commission, and I told them, "I don't know how much time I'm taking off. So if you want me to do work for you, please ask. I'll let you know if I'm not ready." When my daughter was just ten weeks old, she slept through the night, and I felt like a real human being because I was also getting enough sleep! The clients started calling me about that time, and I felt comfortable accepting a few projects. I quickly found that I couldn't work when she was sleeping during the day, as I kept checking on her every few seconds or looking over at every sigh and snore. I didn't want her to go to a day care, so I found and hired a part-time nanny. She started off just two mornings a week, and within a year she was working half days every weekday. She was with us for over three years, working five to six hours a day by the end. She was a part-time college student, and because my work schedule was flexible, I was able to accommodate her changing class schedule each semester.

The part-time nanny solution was an excellent middle way for me. It gave me the chance do work that I really enjoy and maintain the business I had spent fifteen years building! I felt happy contributing to our household income, too. I was very pleased that my daughter got loving, individual care in our home, and I still had plenty of time to be with her. Our nanny was thrilled to find a job that worked with her changing school schedule. It wasn't the cheapest option, by any means, but it worked very well and was worth it, in my mind.

My husband made a key point that stuck with me. He pointed out that if I was going to hire a nanny so I could work, I had to be sure that my business would make a profit over and above the expense of child care—not just earn enough for the nanny, which would equate working for my own sanity. This helped me choose higher-paying projects and be efficient with my available working time, and I was able to turn a profit!

Set your office space up so it's child-friendly.

• Use baby gates to close your child into your office space with you so you don't have to worry about their safety.
• Consider using a sling-type carrier so that you can wear your infant while you work.
• Put an infant swing and/or bassinet in your office.
• Have toys in your office so your child can play next to you while you work.
• Childproof important office equipment (e.g., desktop computer, printer) to avoid financial loss and confrontations with your toddler.

Alternatively, if you have in-home or out-of-home child care, *let your office be your sacred work space* so that you can be effective. If your child doesn't see the office as fun play space, they won't bother you as much there.

Schedule time to regularly get out of the office *without your child* so that you can decompress. We all love our children, and sometimes we love them a little more if we have a break. Being a parent (especially with a new baby or toddler) is exhausting. Don't apologize for needing a break!

This section (and the next ones) make a core assumption: that your child or children don't have extra needs that require attending. Obviously, if you have an exceptional child, you may have a lot more caregiving duties than do most other parents. Following is a vignette from my colleague Mary Sproles Martin.

★★★

Words of Wisdom
from Mary Sproles Martin

For a number of years, I had taken freelance editing as a side project in addition to my full-time salaried position and part-time work as an adjunct English instructor. When my second child, a son, was born eighteen years ago with numerous medical complications, I continued to work this mishmash as much as possible. It soon became apparent that I could not continue to teach. Luckily, I could communicate with the publications staff of my full-time job and hit deadlines from the hospital or from home—wherever my most pressing needs landed me. A change in upper management forced me out a few years later.

This decision shook my confidence. I was a single mother with three children under age eight. It took me nearly a decade to fully accept that it was not a personal failure or the result of any shortcoming on my part. The journal for which I had been editing remains my steadiest client, and I have woven numerous projects in (and out) over the subsequent years.

There are times when I have to completely focus on the medical issues at hand. There is only so much that can be accomplished with any sort of accuracy under conditions of tremendous stress and sleep deprivation. Somehow, through perseverance and renewed searching, work comes, the mortgage is paid, food is on the table.

WHEN THERE ARE SCHOOL-AGE CHILDREN AT HOME

Once your kids are school age, they can take care of themselves a lot better and are on a regular, moderately predictable schedule.

Take Our Daughters and Sons to Work Day
falls on the fourth Thursday in April in the United States. Freelancers and self-employed parents know that we have the rare privilege of showing our children how we function in a workplace of our own choosing, creating a career or business based on personal choices and on our own terms. This is a powerful message to impart with actions and words, and it's not limited to just one day a year.

Plan your work around your children's school hours and schedule.
School days come with a regular schedule and predictable breaks, which means you can adopt the same time frames for your business.

- Work during school hours. Maximize your productive time while the kids are otherwise engaged. Try grouping your most time- and brain-intensive tasks for when you have quiet time for concentration and productivity. Then you can reserve lower-concentration tasks (answering email, updating finances, working on social media, errands) for after the kids are home or during their after-school activities.

- Investigate after- and before-school care options or call on family members for child care if you need full days to work. Emergency backup care is particularly important when your child inevitably comes home with the flu or a stomach bug and needs to recuperate—but your work deadlines won't wait.

- Consider setting aside one or two afternoons as "family fun time" when you and your kids can enjoy spending time together.

- If you chose freelancing or self-employment specifically so that you could be an active parent after school hours, then keep that time sacred for being with your kids.

- School holidays, summer break, and track-out times (intersession) are known long in advance, so you can plan your own breaks and vacations around the school schedule. Knowing the planned breaks is also useful when evaluating your workload and accepting new projects or clients.

> If your child goes to year-round school, you are familiar with the track-in/track-out system, in which your child will be in school for six to nine weeks, followed by two to three weeks off. Lots of organizations offer track-out day camps or even at-school care (without classes). This can be a great opportunity for your child to explore interests such as sports, music, or science while you continue to work if you can't take the time off. Alternatively, you can take advantage of intersession to reduce your own schedule and get some quality parenting time or a family vacation.

Have everyone in the family put all important work and personal appointments on a family calendar. Negotiate solutions to scheduling conflicts ahead of time. Give family members advance notice of business conference calls and meetings so they can give you the necessary quiet time or stay off the Internet if you have a video conference that takes up a lot of bandwidth.

Invest in a laptop (if you don't already have one) so that you can take your children to after-school activities and events and get work done while you wait for them.

Go over work time protocols with your children:

- You are the only person allowed to answer your business phone.
- When you need quiet for business calls, they must leave your office and do quiet activities until the call is done.
- If you need to Skype or video conference, no one should do bandwidth-heavy Internet things (streaming videos, etc.).
- Schedule long conference calls while your children are at school.

Even better, *get your kids to hold you accountable!* Offer a reward if they help you stay on task: "If you can be quiet and take care of yourself for thirty more minutes—and you can tell me to stop when that time is up—while I draft this blog post, then we can go out for ice cream!" You might be surprised at how cooperative children can be in such cases. It also engages them and involves them in your business, so they respect what you do.

Take periodic breaks to spend time with your kids so they don't pester you because they think you're inaccessible, and because they're your kids and you love them.

- Read a book together.
- Get up and dance around the house.
- Make a Lego creation or work on an arts and crafts project.
- Take a short walk.
- Make a picnic snack in the backyard—it doesn't have to be fancy!

Be available for questions at homework time; choose tasks that are less concentration-intensive during this time. Consider having your children sit next to you at your desk to do their homework, to make quick consultations easier and to have parent-child companionship. Having a consistent time each day to do homework—especially if you're also working—establishes strong study habits for students.

Homeschooling is growing in popularity as an educational option. It may sound impossible to balance self-employment with homeschooling—especially if you're the teacher *and* the business owner. But it is possible. My colleague April Michelle Davis balances freelancing with homeschooling, and she graciously shares her experience, choices, and schedule.

Words of Wisdom
from April Michelle Davis

Before becoming self-employed or starting a family, I had worked in the public school system. I learned from that experience that I wanted to homeschool my child. I began to homeschool my son when he turned three. I prepared and made lessons for him based on his interests and age-appropriateness. At age five, we began working through a set curriculum. We have lessons year round, so our daily lesson time is relatively minimal.

In addition to the homeschool curriculum, my son takes Spanish via Skype and gymnastics lessons. I have learned to plan what to work on before I sit at my desk, so that when he is having Spanish lessons I can quickly begin working. Having a smart phone allows me to read emails at any moment in the day, and having a WiFi hot spot on my phone allows me to work with my laptop no matter where I am.

My husband works from home as well and can be available to help as needed. If I have a large project or a rush deadline, he will schedule a day off and care for our son. I have trained my son so that I can now talk on the phone with clients while he is in the room; he understands that there are times when I must work while he quietly plays nearby.

I work full time for my business, so I complete my workday when my son goes to his room at 8:00 p.m., with my husband on caregiving duties until morning. I work a few more hours and then get to sleep, waking by 8:00 a.m., ready for another joyous day.

WHEN THERE ARE TEENS IN YOUR OFFICE

Who are these young adults in your home, and what did they do with your babies?! Kids grow up—shockingly fast—and teenagers bring a whole new set of parental concerns and time commitments.

Talk to your teens about the advantages and disadvantages of self-employment. You're setting an example for them as workers. We are taught from a young age to "find" or "get" a job. You have a unique opportunity to show your teens how to create one's own job!

When I quit my job to be a full-time freelancer at age twenty-four, I was terrified. I didn't know anyone who had done that, so I felt like I had no role models. But then I realized I had a shining example right in front of me: my mother. She is a CPA and had alternately been a partner in a small firm or entirely self-employed, running her practice from a full home office. In fact, she was my first boss: she hired me (and later my sister) to answer phones, make copies, and assemble tax returns. She and my father instilled a strong work ethic in me, and watching her run her own business showed me it could be done on my terms. This gave me a huge boost of confidence as I created my own career.

Ask your teens to take on some office tasks (and pay them). This lightens your workload, teaches your child about work and dependability, and allows your teen to feel useful and earn money. Engaging them with your business can instill in them a sense of pride in their own work, inspiration, and satisfaction with work well done. It can teach them good habits for work: showing up as agreed, doing the work asked of them, doing their best, and even creative thinking if they can come up with solutions you haven't thought of!

> There are some tax benefits to hiring your under-age-eighteen child: their wages are exempt from Social Security, Medicare, and federal unemployment taxes, up to certain limits, if you're operating as a sole proprietorship (always check current tax regulations and rules for these exemptions). Their pay is also a business write-off for you in a way that reduces your tax bill.

Discuss office-hours behavior with your teens. Will it break your concentration if their friends hang out in your home while you're working? Their phone conversations should not take place in your hearing range, so you can concentrate. Their Internet time should not be so bandwidth-intensive that your computer work slows to a crawl. Teens are starting to stretch their independence (and sometimes test the limits), so these items may need to be negotiated, instead of just laying down the law (although in some cases you have to enforce the rules rather strictly). You may need to adjust your schedule to do phone conversations while they are at school or otherwise occupied. A little give-and-take in making compromises respects their growing personhood and choice making.

If your teens have part-time jobs (that are not with your business), talk with them about how they will get to work and who needs the family vehicles at which times. Again, this may be a negotiation or compromise.

If you have to drive them back and forth to jobs or other activities (sports, music, etc.), then get your laptop and park at the coffee shop or library while they are occupied.

Again, if you chose freelancing or self-employment specifically to have the flexibility to spend time with your kids while they are not in school, then make use of that schedule to be involved with what they are doing. Keep in mind that most teens are seeking independence and want to be on their own (or with their friends) a lot more than they did before. Don't be hurt by this—it's part of growing up.

A NOTE ABOUT FOUR-LEGGED KIDS

Carving out time for pet care can also affect your working schedule. Obedience training, dog walking and play time, rescuing animals, senior pet care—all of these can place demands on our time. Sometimes our pets think we work at home solely for their entertainment! But many of the tips in this chapter apply to caring for pets as well as children. My colleague Amy J. Schneider offers some thoughts about freelancing and pet care in the vignette on the following page.

Words of Wisdom
from Amy J. Schneider

I don't have children, but my house is plenty full: currently three dogs, four cats, and a parakeet. The dogs take up the greatest amount of my time. The puppy years are the most demanding, with frequent walks, training, play time, socialization, extra vet trips for puppy shots and neutering, and so on—similar to the infant and toddler years for children. In recent years, I also had an elderly dog with geriatric issues at the other end of the life cycle, and the extra care that entailed. One of the perks of freelancing is that I'm home and can be flexible enough to deal with a busy puppy (or a fragile older dog); with my husband's demanding work schedule, I'm not sure we could do it otherwise. The payoff for the extra work (in addition to the knowledge that the crazy puppy will eventually became a mature, well-trained couch potato) comes in walk and play breaks between chapters, social opportunities for both of us at training classes and play dates, and the fact that every day is Take Your Dog to Work Day.

CHAPTER 6

Working and Caring
for Elderly Parents

Many people today find themselves in the sandwich generation: responsible for children and caring for aging parents at the same time. Many who don't have kids (or they are out of the house) are involved in elder care for family members. There are some parallels with child care—appointments, activities, arranging a schedule—but different dynamics and different concerns. Following are some general tips for keeping your business going while serving as a caregiver.

- Set things up so that you can work both from your home and from your parent's home, if you need to be there. Some people have enough room to move in family members and not have to travel between homes, which can be convenient.

- In your home and in your parent's home, keep handy an updated list of your parent's health care providers and their contact information, plus all medications and dosages.

- Educate yourself on whatever conditions your parent has. This book is by no means a guide on how to become a caregiver or a manual on medical conditions. The point here is that if you are knowledgeable in these areas, you can see what will be needed of you as a caregiver, and then how you can make it work with your business.

- Aides are available (part time or more) to help with your parent's care, particularly if you're not comfortable or skilled with certain tasks.

- Investigate local day programs or respite care programs for a parent with dementia or a similar condition.

- Have frank talks with other family members about your parent's care needs and arrange for nearby relatives to help so that you can get work done.

- Arrange with neighbors to rotate take-a-meal-to-your-neighbors nights. This gives you relief from being responsible for everything all the time and some interaction with friends.

My friend and colleague Dawn McIlvain Stahl made adjustments to her freelance career after a family member's medical catastrophe. She graciously shares her experience (which follows in some length, as she has many valuable lessons).

Words of Wisdom
from Dawn McIlvain Stahl

Unlike freelancing, which was preceded by a layoff that was long in coming, caregiving wasn't something I had time to prepare for. My mom, a young-for-her-age fifty-nine-year-old, survived a nearly unsurvivable stroke a few years ago.

I was relatively mobile, already comfortable working on my laptop and phone for long stretches. But there was nothing comfortable (or particularly commendable) about the mediocre work and poor client communications that occurred during the long stretches at the sides of hospital and nursing home beds in the first several months, except that my mom— and my career—lived through it.

Mom uses a wheelchair now, is dominant-side paralyzed, and has some short-term memory loss and motor/muscle control issues. She's sweet and hilarious but requires full-time care. My dad is her primary caregiver, with me as the secondary. We use a shared Google spreadsheet to plan the caregiver schedule and a purple notebook and binder as a daily record (medicine, nutrition, other trends) and as a catchall for our caregiver notes. It's not the most sophisticated system, but it works. When it comes to work-life-caregiving balance, I believe strongly in systems.

The system I use for work is called "grouping" (or "the rodeo" when it's feeling like barely controlled chaos): I group together complementary, same-brain work tasks and try to schedule one-off tasks or low-key research and background work for times when I'm most likely to be interrupted. For example, I try to edit a solid batch of articles in one afternoon session, run cleanup macros and searches on several Chicago-style book chapters in one evening session, and leave things like answering email, scanning Feedly for copyediting-relevant articles, or doing photo research for blog posts for brief bouts of downtime while I'm caregiving.

I have routinely reminded myself that I will only accomplish about half as much as I think I will whenever I'm trying to multitask—working and caregiving at the same time—but I'm routinely disappointed in how little I get done during these sessions. It would be better if I stopped trying to overlap the two, but until I have that much unitasking self-control, I settle for not doing any tight-deadline work when I'm actively caregiving. Because therein lies disaster—or at least work- and relationship-damaging stress.

For the most part, I've always grouped work in the way I've described here, finding it to be the most efficient method for tackling the diverse tasks that make up my business. The biggest adjustment I've made, and also the most significant trade-off, has been the volume of work I do. I also look at metrics differently. Whereas I previously judged my freelance success on one simple metric—income replacement (my freelance income needed to be equal to or greater than my in-house income), with a bonus given for working on "important academic materials"—I now place a higher value on doing work in a kind, conscientious, and competent manner. I don't think it's a coincidence that those are also the qualities I strive for in my caregiving efforts.

Thankfully, I'm in a position to make that trade—exchanging some work volume, income, and prestige for the satisfaction of helping with my mom's care while also providing valuable services to a variety of clients. I've realized that our patchwork caregiving system is working fairly well, and I could increase the volume of larger projects that I take on. I was somewhat surprised to realize that I don't really want to. I'm filling in the open edges of time with things like taking the dog on longer walks and trying some new recipes.

Achieving a work-caregiving balance was at times a shockingly difficult process. But after three and a half years, I'm recognizing (with cautious optimism) that it has had a tremendously valuable outcome: it has forced me to learn how to better balance work and life in general. If that ever seems like too little reward for the required effort, I only have to hear my mom laugh at some pun or word-related goofiness to know that it has been well worth it.

CHAPTER 7

Making Time and Space
For *You*

It seems that when we are self-employed and balancing the needs of our business with the needs of our families and other obligations, the first thing to go is time for our personal interests and self-care. When a deadline is looming, your kids need shuttling to various activities, the house needs cleaning (always), and you've got a long list of errands, the last thing you think of doing is taking a personal break. I've said it before, and it bears repeating: **You are important, and you should make yourself a priority, without apology.**

Carving out time for yourself needs to happen when you are planning your time and tasks (refer to chapter 2 for some task management tips). In addition to laying out your work tasks and obligations, put your personal wants and needs in the plan! Your needs and desires should be treated as bit of a priority, not just as an afterthought you tack on or squeeze in here and there.

GOOD HEALTH

Taking care of yourself physically—with exercise, good eating, proper rest, and whatever self-care activities you need—is necessary just to maintain good health, but it seems many self-employed people work hard enough to push our bodies to the breaking point. Chronic stress over long periods can have a devastating effect on one's health. One of the harsh truths about freelancing and self-employment: there is no paid sick time. Working through physical pain or illness may be necessary from time to time. If the health crisis is more severe, you may be forced to take time off or turn down work for some time.

- When accepting work, projects, and new clients, try to build in some "life happens" time in the schedule. When you're working the hardest seems to be when you're most vulnerable to whatever flu bug is going around or manage to injure yourself.

- Take care of yourself with daily routines: drinking plenty of fluids, getting exercise, eating healthy meals, and so on. When you practice a routine enough, it becomes a habit, something you do automatically that requires little effort.

Building a Habit

It takes about thirty days of daily effort to make a new habit. If you want to add habits like regular meditation, a writing discipline, or exercise to your daily routine, plan to keep at it at least a month for it to become ingrained.

- Support your body with proper ergonomics—a good chair, lumbar support, foot support, wrist rests, and so on. If you need wrist braces, gloves, or other support, invest in them and use them as needed to stay healthy and strong. See chapter 9 for more suggestions on supporting your body while working.

- Make care of your body a priority. It's easy to fall into the trap of thinking about doctor appointments as a loss of time and money. Think of them instead as an *investment* in your health. Regular checkups and treatments for specific issues (e.g., physical therapy) can prevent major problems down the line. Chiropractic, acupuncture, and other holistic methods can keep you healthy and strong.

• If you're overworked but the end is in sight, schedule something nice for yourself, like a massage or spa treatment. Not only will you be relaxing after a tough time, you have created a dangling carrot for getting your work done!

You will occasionally get sick or injured and have to scale back your work or stop entirely for a while. See chapter 8 on work emergencies for ideas on planning ahead and coping. Adrienne Montgomerie shares some of her experiences of keeping a business running after injuries that had a lasting effect.

Words of Wisdom
from Adrienne Montgomerie

When you are sick or injured, you do not do your best work. Your mind is not clear, your energy is not high. Some injuries, such as a concussion, can really suffer when you try to work, causing your recovery time to increase exponentially. Other sicknesses (a head cold or sprained wrist) require just a little downtime or accommodation.

When I was hit by a car, I went AWOL for a couple of days. When I remembered to call my clients, I gave a quick explanation of what happened (because I didn't want to seem like a flake who couldn't handle life's little ups and downs), and they encouraged me to reduce my workload to take time to recover. (This considerate approach quickly moved those clients to the top of my favorites list, and I have since bent over backward to accommodate them and give them the best service available.)

I tried to work when I was in pain but quickly realized that I was not up to my usual quality. I moved some responsibilities to assistants and distributed some of the work to others. When I got a bad concussion (does this make me seem accident prone?), I could barely think of a sentence, let alone edit one. I tried to work rather than giving my brain the "complete rest" that is advised as treatment. It took six months before I felt that I could think clearly and two years before I felt like my old self.

Recognize that you may have lingering effects of an illness or injury that affect your work. My first concussion (I've had more than one) gave me a kind of blindness to my own mistakes. I had to learn cognitive strategies and new tech tools to compensate for this (very helpful things to learn, it turns out). I did not offer my core services until I was fully recovered (two years), focusing instead on related services and writing and teaching.

VOLUNTEER WORK

Do you volunteer your time, skills, and energies? Volunteering is a terrific way to get involved with issues you care about and give of yourself and your talents (not just your money). Depending on where and how you volunteer, it might lead to more business opportunities because you can meet people who need your professional skills.

- Set aside a specific time each week when you will do the volunteer work, if it's regular. For instance, if you lead a scout troop, you might schedule a specific time slot each week in which you prepare for and arrange meetings and activities. Then, of course, you'll have the meetings and activities to attend!

- If your volunteer activity occurs in bursts (election campaigns, a fund-raiser event like a 5K race), put it on the calendar well in advance and arrange your workload to accommodate it.

- Don't say yes to *every* volunteer opportunity, or you will be overwhelmed. Ask yourself the yes/no questions that appear in chapter 1 when evaluating whether to raise your hand when volunteers are called for. Think about what opportunities feed your core values or are most important to you.

- If a volunteer opportunity doesn't give you something or reflect your values in some way, reconsider whether it's the right fit for you. If or when it becomes a chore, just another obligation, then it might be time to let it go.

HOBBIES, SPORTS, AND OTHER ACTIVITIES

Doing things that interest you—volunteer work, involvement in church or faith community, sports or physical activity, traveling, or spending time working on your hobbies—takes you out of your work head, which is mentally healthy. Even if we love what we do, we can't do it around the clock to the exclusion of everything else. There has to be a mental break. It can leave you feeling refreshed and more energetic. It feeds the other parts of you that need attention.

A creative hobby (knitting, quilting, jewelry making, woodworking, acting, music performance) is a great way to express yourself and have some "you" time. I find that quilting is a terrific balance to my work: a way to be creative without words. New research is showing that creative hobbies keep the mind sharp as we age. Hobbies like knitting are very portable. So many freelancers and self-employed people are engaged in knowledge work that doesn't necessarily result in a physical product. Making something with our hands and creativity can be a fulfilling counterbalance to that. Musical performances, acting, and traveling may not create a physical object but can inspire us to live in the moment by making great memories and a powerful experience.

Sports and other physical activity can be a great way to stay healthy, reduce stress, and have fun and can be a particularly good counterbalance to work that might require you to sit still at a computer all day! Whether you prefer to be active on your own—perhaps swimming, running, or yoga—or with a group, be sure to make exercise a priority in your schedule if it's important to you. Many self-employed folks end up being isolated by working solo, and thus finding a class, group, or exercise buddy can be a great way to get out, be sociable, and do things you enjoy with others.

In the following vignette, world traveler and web design guru Leandra Simpson Ganko shares how she manages a business while hitting the road.

Words of Wisdom
from Leandra Simpson Ganko

My husband and I love to travel, but I also need to deliver projects to my web design business clients on time. Working from anywhere is easy with a laptop, reliable WiFi, and a universal plug adapter, but the real key is work-life balance. One of my main strategies is to be very transparent about my frequent trips. I give my ongoing clients advance warning of when I will be traveling so we can plan work, and I never schedule website launches right before I leave in case I need to troubleshoot issues.

We get stir-crazy if we don't hit the skies (usually internationally) about seven or eight times a year, sometimes for a week or longer. I rarely work in-flight, instead using downtime during layovers in airport lounges to catch up on news and complete simple tasks. We also book hotels with complimentary WiFi (if possible), and my smart phone plan includes free data and texting in over 150 countries.

While I am away from the home office, I monitor my email and respond to new inquiries or let clients know I am aware of their questions; otherwise, I let the away message speak for me so I can explore the streets of southern Spain or relax on a beach in Thailand!

Part 3

BALANCE CORRECTION

There are times when your work-life balance will be way out of whack. This is normal! Sometimes it is *supposed* to be unbalanced—like when you have a baby or move to a new house. As I mentioned earlier, life balance is not something you achieve once and lock into forever; you will be doing constant course correction. This part covers planning for emergencies, dealing with being overworked, and filling time when you don't have enough to do.

CHAPTER 8

Planning Ahead for
For Work Emergencies

No matter how healthy, well organized, carefully scheduled, or prepared you are, emergencies will fall into your life. All kinds of things can derail you: a broken bone (yours or a family member's), the flu, a missed flight, death in the family, computer crash, natural disaster, car breakdown, and so on. Even good things can wreck the schedule: planned trips, holidays, and kids being off from school. Sometimes you get a whole string of small crises that pile on to make a mess of your plans. Some emergencies are small and easily handled, and others are large and unwieldy. Some planning can help you avert major panic and have systems in place to support you. Reducing anxiety can go a long way toward keeping or restoring a healthy work-life balance.

QUICK ACCESS

Maintain a list of current projects, with contact information and project deadlines, in a quickly accessible file, folder, or database on your computer (and/or in the cloud, in case your computer crashes) so that adult family members can notify project owners if you're incapacitated. A desktop shortcut works well. You could use a password-protected file if you want to be secure.

Periodically remind your life partner or another adult you trust *where to find information about your business in an emergency*. Whether they have full or limited access to your files and programs, they should know what to do (or be easily instructed). Several times I have called my husband and said, "Please go to my desktop, go into my email, and send a message to <client> that reads 'Laura is on a business trip and will review those files when she returns on Monday.'" (I've had to do this when I was unable to respond to email for some reason while traveling, which is rarely a problem anymore.) He's also had to email files to me.

Communicate with your clients. If you cultivate good working relationships with your clients (something you should do all the time, not just in an emergency), you can contact them when you're having troubles and work something out. You should feel comfortable asking for deadline extensions, options for completing work, or even handing back an unfinished project if necessary. Up-front communication about delays and issues is always appreciated. You don't have to spin a giant sob story to get sympathy, and in fact, you might keep the details minimal to appear professional.

PROTECT YOUR DIGITAL ASSETS

Make backups. Sometimes the crisis is a computer crash, hard drive failure, virus, or corrupted file. Make sure you regularly and securely back up your files and system. Whether you go with external hard drives or cloud-based storage, be *certain* that you can get your files when needed. It only takes one catastrophe to drive home the need for this. I once inadvertently deleted a file that had six weeks' worth of work in it, and it could *not* be recovered, even by my computer tech husband. At the time, I didn't do regular backups. I called the client, literally in tears, and we figured out what to do, and then I immediately bought an external drive and now run daily backups, which has already paid off more than once. (Better yet, buy two drives and rotate between your desk and an off-site location, such as a friend's house or your safe-deposit box, as insurance against theft or acts of God on your house.)

Get an uninterruptible power supply (UPS). A UPS system will give you a few minutes (or longer) of power in an outage, giving you time to save work, close files, and safely shut down. They often have surge protectors built right in to protect from dangerous power spikes. Some power suppliers (especially in rural areas) have nearly daily quick power outages (a flicker, aka "dirty power"), and having a UPS can prevent stress headaches over lost work.

WORKING YOUR SCHEDULE

Review your calendar carefully when accepting work. For instance, imagine you are offered a project that would normally take you about five weeks to complete, but the client is asking for it in four weeks. You aren't fully loaded with projects, so you figure you can get it done in that time frame. But when you check the calendar, you realize your kids are tracked out of school for two of those weeks, which usually means you're shuttling them around to various camps and activities, eating significant portions of your workday. Then you have to decide whether you're going to try to do it in the allotted time anyway and work really hard to finish before the kids are out of school (possibly overworking yourself), ask for an extended deadline, or pass on the project altogether.

When you're scheduling projects, *try to build in some extra "life happens" time.* Remember that nothing ever goes perfectly as planned. People get sick or hurt, storms knock out power, cars break down, construction projects always run over schedule. Obviously, we can't anticipate every disaster, but a little extra schedule padding frequently pays off.

When you must accompany family members to appointments or events but still need to work, *take a laptop with you.* It can be a pain to drag work with you wherever you go, but from time to time, it must be done. Sometimes, an hour (or a half hour, or just fifteen minutes) to catch up on emails and social media while out and about can make a big difference in freeing up productive time when you're back in the office.

A Perfect Storm of Bad Luck

In spring 2015, I was working hard on my deadlines and preparing to go to Texas for five days for a quilt show, where I would be taking a workshop and learning some exciting new techniques. I was really excited! Less than a week before the trip, my husband got a kidney stone, a very stubborn one that would not pass. He was in incredible pain, and I took him to the ER four times in six days before he was finally admitted to the hospital for a procedure to remove it. During his pain-filled days, I couldn't concentrate on work very well and didn't get much done. It snowed heavily twice, canceling my daughter's preschool, so then I had an antsy four-year-old at home who wanted entertaining. Obviously, I got almost nothing done. Two days before my scheduled trip, I decided to cancel it. I hadn't finished enough work before leaving, and my husband was still in incredible pain. I hated to miss a pleasure trip, but it was for the right reasons and I don't regret doing it.

One saving grace during this time was my mother. She lives in our neighborhood, and she was able to care for my daughter a lot during those snowy days, including two sleepovers. I was able to call her at 5:30 a.m. and say, "Come over now, I have to take my husband to the ER right away!" My father-in-law also came to spend time with my husband in the hospital while I went home to care for our daughter one night. Family members to the rescue!

CALL IN THE REINFORCEMENTS

Develop a network of colleagues you can ask to pitch in on projects when you have a personal emergency. If you have subcontractors or associates in your business, make sure they know what to do if you need backup. Team collaboration software can make this easier. Much of this is cloud-based now, and you can put relevant details for clients and projects where your team members can access them.

When I was getting ready to have my daughter, I laid out plans as best I could, knowing that I couldn't be entirely sure of what would happen. I stopped accepting work two weeks before my due date and finished up a few odds and ends for a week or so after that. I had one client with parts of a project trickling in, and I let them know that they could continue to contact me but at some point they would get a response saying "Can't work, had a baby!" A colleague covered for me with some of my steadier work. I told my clients I wasn't sure how much time I would take off (because I wasn't sure what my new family would need from me), but they could always ask. My daughter was born about five days before her due date, and very kindly was a good sleeper, so I was rested and ready to work again fairly quickly, once I found a part-time nanny.

Child care plans: This is a big one, especially for self-employed business owners with smaller children. It pays to have reliable plans for child care. Look into after-school care, drop-in care, day camps and other activities, family members babysitting, regular sitters, and emergency sitters you can call in a pinch. Sometimes, despite your best efforts, none of these are available.

CHAPTER 9

When You're Overworked

You *will* overcommit yourself in your business from time to time. Time is money—every project is money, and you get used to having it (and wanting it). No work means no paycheck. When you have trained yourself to say yes to everything, it becomes extremely difficult to say no. Sometimes, even when you've planned appropriately, client needs change, schedules shift, and suddenly you have more to finish on tighter deadlines. Or you get sick or injured, losing working time. So how do you cope when you've got too much to do? Following are some thoughts about getting through the "feast" part of the feast-or-famine cycle.

COPING WITH THE WORK

Get to work and be productive. Work, work, work. Get up early or stay up late. Work weekends and lunch hours. The plus side is this: there is an end to it. Once you meet your deadlines, you can have some time off. You will start to learn how much your optimal workload is, and when you are beyond that level.

On the flip side, *know when you simply can't work anymore.* If it is taking you two hours to read five pages, then you just need to stop and have a break. A twenty-minute nap, a lunch break, or even a half day off can do more for your productivity (and sanity) than ten hours of work if it leaves you refreshed and rested.

Key Point

If you have to work extra hours,
still be aware of when you simply
can't work anymore.

Learn your most effective time of day, and set it aside for work. For me, it's any time before lunch, so I get up early, get into the office, and start right away. For others, it's the afternoon and early evening. Some people (my husband) are night owls and can work well late at night.

At a certain level of stress, you may find yourself zooming through work. I function well with two or three larger projects at a time, with smaller ones coming in and going out. Pay attention to when you feel most effective and make note of your work levels. Also pay attention to when you start to feel overworked, so you can identify those times (and maybe take steps to prevent them).

Head down, blinders on. Turn off instant messaging, turn off the TV, and don't check email or Facebook every five minutes (better yet, use a social media blocker, like a Pomodoro timer). Ignore the phone unless it's an emergency. You may need to let those around you know that you won't be very responsive.

Triage your schedule. See the list-making and task management techniques in chapter 2. If you need more hours for work, then look at what other items can be deleted, deferred until later, or delegated to someone else (the three D's in chapter 2). I start by looking at what appointments might be deleted (e.g., networking groups), and then at what tasks I can delegate to my virtual assistant.

Be aware of your deadlines and time. It's tempting to say yes to every new project, but you don't always have time to complete them. Make sure you don't have five deadlines all on the same day or accept a rush job that you don't really have time for.

Get help. Find some subcontractors, associates, or colleagues to help you finish a project. If family members (including kids) are willing and able, enlist them to help (for pay, if necessary). If you can't get help in the office (obviously, not all work can just be passed on to someone else), get help with the rest of your life: grocery delivery, cleaning service, cooking, and so on.

SUPPORT YOUR BODY

When you're working double time to complete projects, your body can certainly pay the price. Here are some ideas to keep you physically functioning and productive.

- Rest your eyes, stretch your legs, and move around during the day. Too much sitting in front of the computer can be bad for you in a number of ways.

- Use topical gels or take painkillers when your wrists and hands start to hurt (they will) from using the computer too much.

- Look up every twenty minutes and focus on objects at a distance or take walks to rest your eyes (you can ruin your long-distance vision with too much reading; I speak from experience).

- Make sure your office setup is comfortable. Invest in a drafting table or a standing-height table if you can; it is well worth the money and will pay for itself by helping you avoid the chiropractor.

- Invest in supports to keep your body comfortable: ergonomic chair, wrist pads, arm support, lumbar support, foot rest, even heating pads if necessary. When you're overworked and in pain, take pain relievers and any other medications you need to support your body.

- Use music and sounds to create a supportive environment. I play nature sounds, minimalist orchestral music, cheerful piano music, or works by my favorite composers when I need to be very focused and productive.

- It's easy to binge on junk food for quick energy bursts, so try to have healthy eating and drinking options available.

- Try to get enough sleep to stay clearheaded and focused. As I mentioned earlier, a quick nap can do worlds of good for your productivity when you're stressed out.

- Find time for simple, quick stress relievers: a ten-minute walk in your neighborhood, meditation, a few yoga poses or tai chi movements, a cuddle with your kids or significant other, a phone call with a friend, a hot cup of tea, even a calming scented candle can give you a mental refresher.

WHEN YOU'RE FINISHED

Once you survive a period of stressful overwork, take a break. Rest and recharge. Step back and appreciate what you managed to do. Detox from the adrenaline and recuperate.

Give yourself a reward for finishing! Sometimes knowing you have a treat coming can be motivating when the work is piled on. I love a pedicure or a massage after a difficult week. Coffee with friends or a walk in a park can be just the stress reliever one needs. Spa day? New set of golf clubs? Whatever it takes! Dangle that carrot so you can carry on and finish.

Once you've caught your breath, look back at your busy time and examine it. If you ask yourself the following questions, you can harvest some valuable insights that can inform how you work in the future, hopefully smoothing out the feast-or-famine cycle and allowing you to work at your preferred rate.

- How did you get so busy all at once? Did deadlines slip? Is your work seasonal with defined times of extra tasks? Did you say yes to too many things?

- Did anything go wrong in the work that fouled up the schedule? If so, what was it, and how did it go wrong?

- Did anything unexpected come up (say, a health crisis) that interfered? Was it within your control or not? How could you plan and cope for this in the future?

- What improved your productivity? What hampered it?

- What did you get accomplished? How will that accomplishment affect your business?

- What did it cost you (not just money but time, energy, relationships) to get this work done?

- How could I have completed this work more smoothly? What choices did I make that affected the workload?

- How can I prevent getting overworked like that again? What choices are within my power to make to shape my business toward what I want?

- What coping strategies worked, and what didn't? What else could I try in the future?

The point of these questions is to learn from the stress and make changes so that you don't get into a vicious feast-or-famine cycle or, worse, become constantly overworked. Many self-employed people don't like being overworked, but we get into an adrenaline cycle and can't seem to stop. Whether we like the extra money or the feeling of being productive, or we just can't say no when we should, we periodically take on too much. Some people become chronically overworked because they don't learn any lessons from stressful times. This is ultimately unsustainable. If you are thoughtful in your choices, learn from the tough times, and are bold enough to make changes when needed, you will create the more balanced life you seek.

CHAPTER 10

When You're Underworked

Self-employment and freelance work seems to come in waves—periods of lots of work, then some time of little or no work. Fret not! You can still do things to help your business even when you don't have much billable work in hand. Here are my tips for making use of a slow period. These address the "famine" part of the feast-or-famine cycle.

First, and most important: *Take time off.* Especially during holidays, it's time for you to visit with family and friends, too! Recharge your batteries, enjoy your life, and take some time for yourself. This is important for staving off burnout. Remind yourself that one of the points of your own business is working (and thus, not working) when you choose. A little R&R can be just the mental and physical refresher you need to come back with renewed energy and vigor. It's not a crime to spend a day goofing off, especially if you have the time in your schedule.

Clean and organize. Did your work space get cluttered up? Receipts lying everywhere? Left the filing until you "had a moment"? Now is your chance! Clean and organize your office space and come back to work with a fresh slate. Purge your email inbox, clean up your hard drive, catch up on the filing. Hang that artwork, vacuum, dust, take out the trash and recycling, create a supportive space for your work.

 Bonus tip: Have you been considering implementing a new system for filing, accounting, a database, contacts, or other business process, or perhaps creating forms that might support your business? Devoting time to setting these up carefully and thoughtfully is a great use of downtime. Also, look at chapter 8, plan for emergencies, and start prepping for the busy times!

Paperwork. Get caught up or even ahead of yourself. Need to update files? Transfer handwritten notes to disk? Catch up on accounting software or online banking? Update log files? It's never too late to get caught up or get a jump start on the year-end paperwork you might need. *Especially important:* Start inputting everything you need to generate some current financial information. Getting your paperwork up to date now saves you tons of time and frustration when taxes are due.

> **Bonus tip:** If you get an accurate picture of your business finances, you'll immediately see where you can make more money, where you can cut expenses, and more opportunities for growth. Don't wait until the end of the year for this!

Set some goals. If you have updated your paperwork (especially finances), you probably have a good picture of what the last year, quarter, or month in your business looked like. Now is a good time to set more yearly, quarterly, and monthly goals for you and your business. Stretch a little! Write the new goals down, so you can track how well you do. Don't wait until the end of the calendar year to set goals—do it now!

> **Bonus tip:** Use downtime to have a business retreat. Spend some dedicated hours brainstorming on your business, making choices on what you want to be doing, and deciding any new directions you want to take. You can have a retreat with colleagues or other freelancers, too—even a virtual retreat, with a day or half day set aside and check-ins via Skype or conference call! I'm usually amazed at what ideas I come up with when I take the time to work on my business this way. A group retreat (or even just pairs of freelancers talking) really inspires creativity!

Learn something. Downtime, even just a few hours, is a terrific time to break out those MP3s you haven't listened to yet, find some books and online training, or read that pile of magazines. It's important to stay current in your field. You'll have the time—so open up your mind and get ready to learn some fabulous new techniques and ideas! Load up your e-reader or your iPod or go to the library. If you don't have a pile of stuff waiting for you, go online to professional associations related to your business.

> **Bonus tip:** When reading, have a notebook handy. If you get inspired by an idea, you can write it down, with reference to where you read it. Then you have a "hot list" of ideas and thoughts that you can refer to without flipping through a pile of material trying to find it again. This can be quite useful when you're searching for blog, article, or speech topics. Alternatively, keep some sticky-note flags available so you can highlight key ideas in a book or magazine.

Update your online presence. You might have a daily or weekly habit of time set aside to maintaining your Facebook page, LinkedIn, Twitter, any other networks you are a member of, and your website. Downtime is a great opportunity to make major updates and changes. LinkedIn particularly is constantly adding new features; take a little time to create a company profile, update your personal profile, find some new groups to join, and ask and answer questions. Write those new pages for your website like you have been thinking about, update your profiles on other sites, and add more content where you can.

> **Bonus tip:** With a social media aggregator, you can write a bunch of status updates and tweets and schedule them to go out in the future, instead of all at once. If you use WordPress for your website, you can draft pages before publishing them, giving you time to work them through carefully and thoughtfully.

Start writing. Write some blog posts, newsletters, articles, even books. When you make your expertise available, you establish yourself as an authority in your subject and offer valuable content to potential customers and clients. Downtime is a great opportunity to let your creative juices flow. Many blogging platforms allow you to schedule the release of your blog posts in advance (I know a professional organizer who has a year's worth of weekly posts already scheduled!). You can easily turn blog posts into articles and publish those on your site (or at a site like http:// ezinearticles.com) or submit them to relevant publications. If you have a regular newsletter, you can start prepping future issues to save time. Finally, you can turn blog posts and articles into speaking presentations (if you have the communication skills), which is a terrific way to build your business. If you have several blog posts, articles, or presentations on a related topic, you have the bulk of a book (or e-book) written.

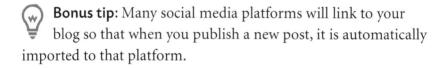 **Bonus tip:** Many social media platforms will link to your blog so that when you publish a new post, it is automatically imported to that platform.

Renew connections and make new ones. Business downtime is a great time to reestablish your professional connections and make new ones. Have lunch, coffee, or meet up with your colleagues and strategic partners. Go through that pile of business cards and connect online (with social media) and in person. Follow up with potential opportunities by calling, sending a handwritten card, or connecting in another way. Find some networking groups to visit and meet new folks.

Bonus tip: Whenever you receive a new business card from a connection, write a note on the back—where and when you met, any key conversation tips you had, when to follow up, or whatever you need to remember the person by more than just a card!

CONCLUSION

As I stated in the introduction, this is book is intended to inspire you to imagine the balance you want, implement the techniques that are relevant for you (or make up some new ones), grow your business, and create the life you dreamed of. I hope you have fresh ideas for creating the work-life balance you seek. Freelancers and self-employed people particularly struggle with this, and the tools, techniques, and stories presented here provide options for you. There is no surefire, one-size-fits-all formula for the perfect life balance, and that's because every person's wants, needs, and obligations are different.

Be bold, make changes, and thrive!

ACKNOWLEDGMENTS

This book grew out of a presentation on creating work-life balance given at the Communication Central conference in Rochester, New York, on September 27, 2014. My co-presenter was Katharine O'Moore-Klopf, who wrote half the outline and primary content with me. She graciously gave her permission for me to develop this book from the presentation, and she contributed whole sections, vignettes, and details from her experience. This book is dedicated to her.

Thanks to Amy J. Schneider for her excellent editorial eye in shaping and cleaning up my prose (no one can edit their own work!). Thanks to Leandra Simpson Ganko, Amy J. Schneider, Dawn McIlvain Stahl, April Michelle Davis, Katharine O'Moore-Klopf, Mary Sproles Martin, and Adrienne Montgomerie for contributing their stories. Thanks especially to Jake Poinier for publishing this book, checking in regularly to see how it was going, and providing data from the *Freelance Forecast* surveys.

ABOUT THE AUTHOR

In 1997, at the age of twenty-four, Laura Poole quit her job to be a full-time freelance copyeditor, founding Archer Editorial Services, Inc. Over years with ups and downs, she managed to keep work coming in; get married, buy a home, and have a baby; and even keep up with her book club, gourmet club, and quilting hobby. She trained to be a professional life coach (earning certification and accreditation), which strongly influenced her perception of a well-balanced life. She enjoys presenting on topics related to the freelance life. She lives in North Carolina with her family.

The Science, Art and Voodoo of
Freelance Pricing and Getting Paid

If you're a freelancer or know a freelancer who thinks, "There's got to be a better way to do this," you're absolutely correct. *The Science, Art and Voodoo of Freelance Pricing and Getting Paid* teaches you the key factors to consider in formulating your pricing and estimates, how to get clients to buy without haggling, sure-fire tips to get slow-pay and no-pay clients in line, and much more!

"Concise, clear, and clever. This excellent guide answered my freelance questions and raised issues I hadn't considered. Helpful to freelancers at all levels."

—AMAZON REVIEW

The Smooth-Sailing Freelancer:
How To Find, Sell, and Retain More Freelance Business

This Dr. Freelance Guide offers strategies for increasing the quality and quantity of your freelance jobs as a writer, editor, graphic designer, web designer, or any other type of entrepreneur in a creative field. *The Smooth-Sailing Freelancer* provides practical, easy-to-implement advice for beginning and intermediate freelancers, as well as veterans who want to do a better job of navigating the freelance waters.

"There's a lot of interesting and helpful information packed into these pages, and it's all well written and beautifully presented. I recommend it to other freelancers."

—AMAZON REVIEW

Help! My Freelancers Are Driving Me Crazy

You want to hire a freelancer who's talented, reliable, flexible and affordable—someone who understands your business needs, has expertise in your industry and hits every deadline. Too much to ask? Not at all. *Help! My Freelancers Are Driving Me Crazy* reveals the keys to driving loyalty and results from your creative workforce, from finding and hiring the right talent, to motivational techniques to incentivize freelancers to perform at a higher level.

"An immensely useful guide for both freelancers and clients that will guide useful conversation. Written in a straightforward way, I found myself dog-earing every other page."

—AMAZON REVIEW

Available from Amazon.com, CreateSpace.com and other retail outlets.

18613907R00056

Printed in Great Britain
by Amazon